Making a rabbit

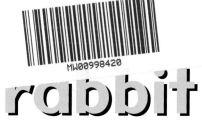

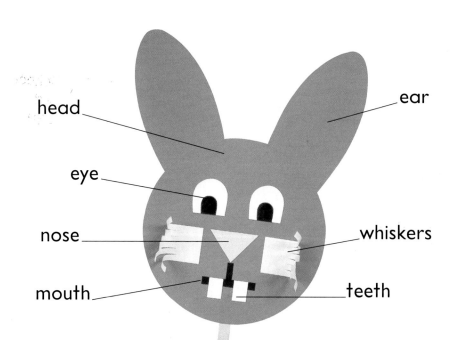

head

ear

eye

nose

whiskers

mouth

teeth

Here is the head.

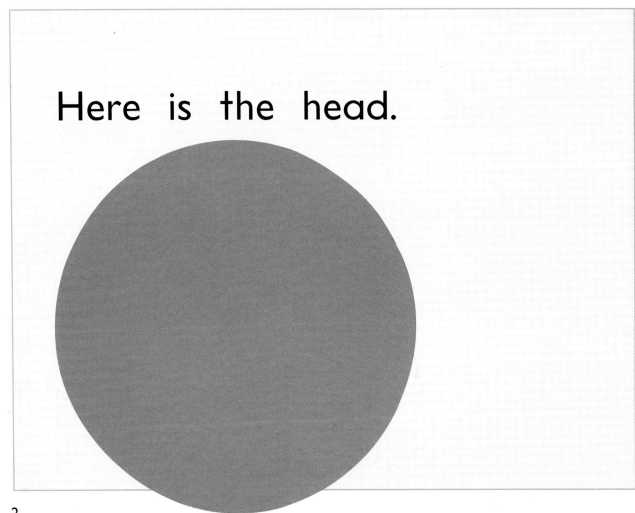

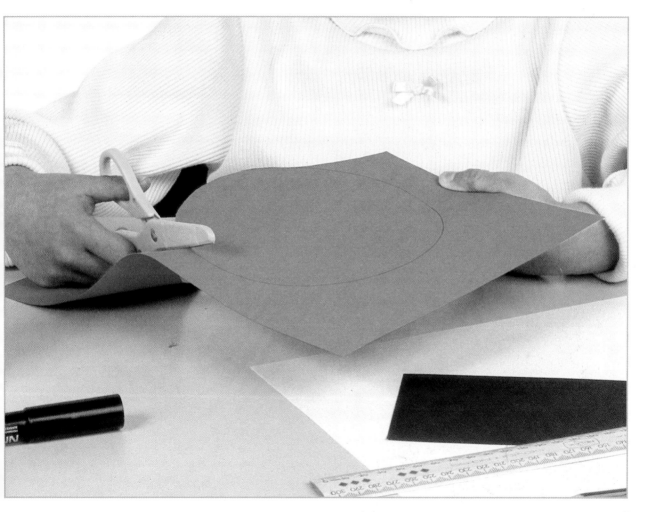

3

Here are the eyes.

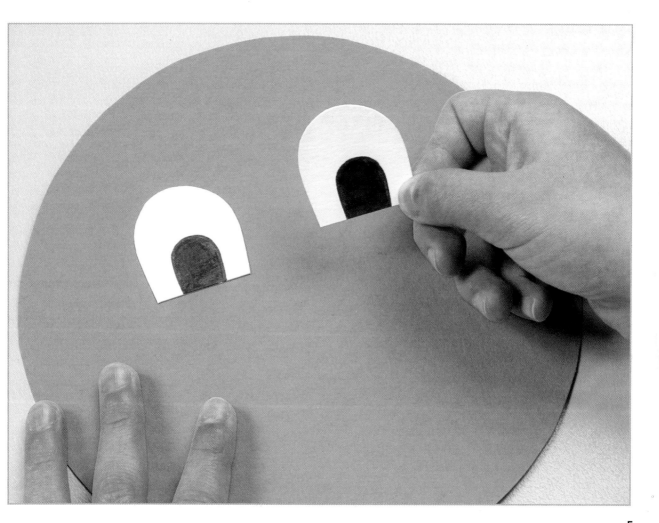

5

Here is the nose.

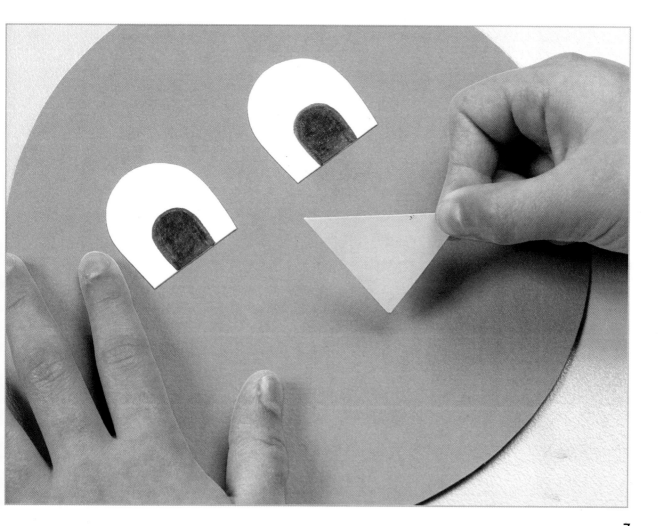

Here are the ears.

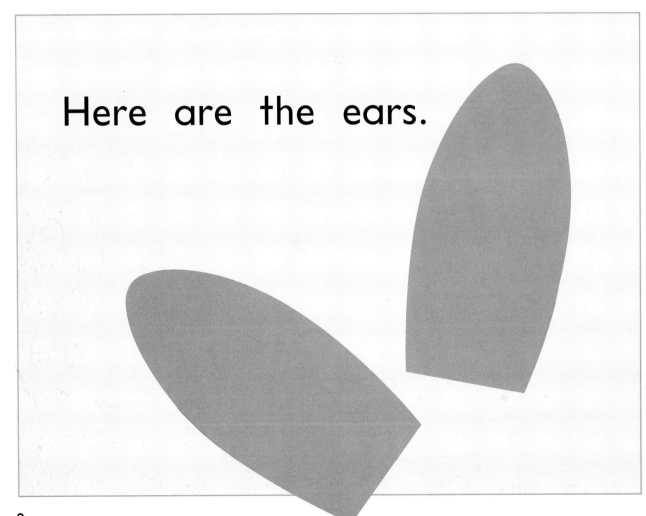

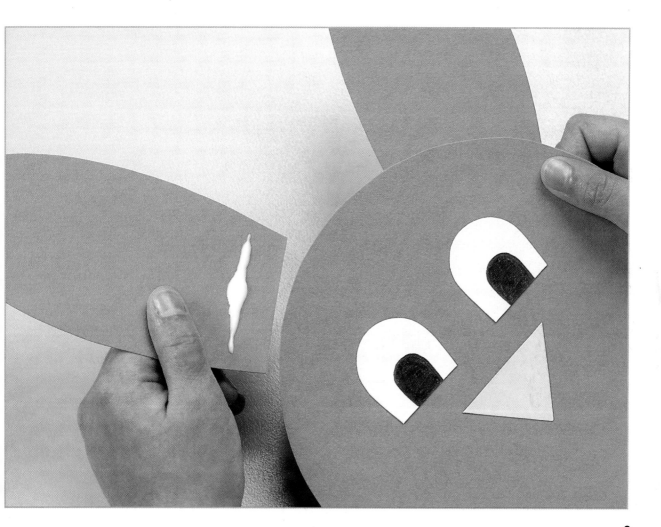

Here is the mouth.

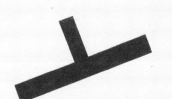

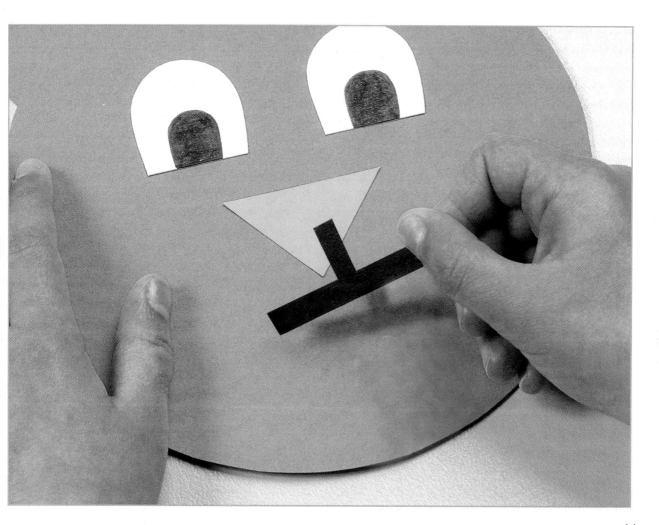

11

Here are the teeth.

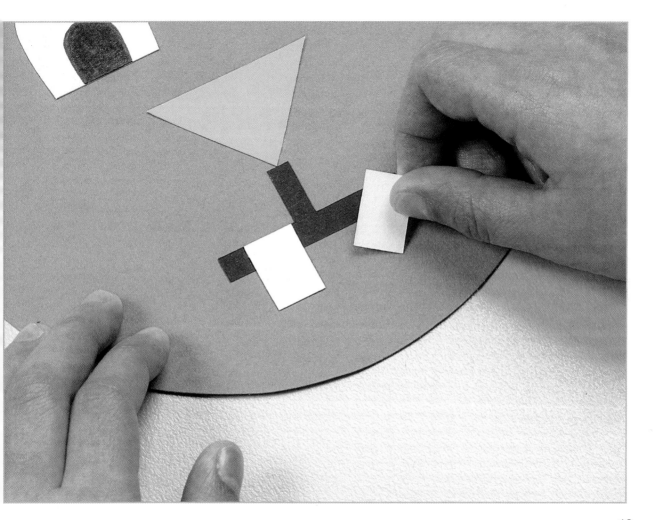

Here are the whiskers.

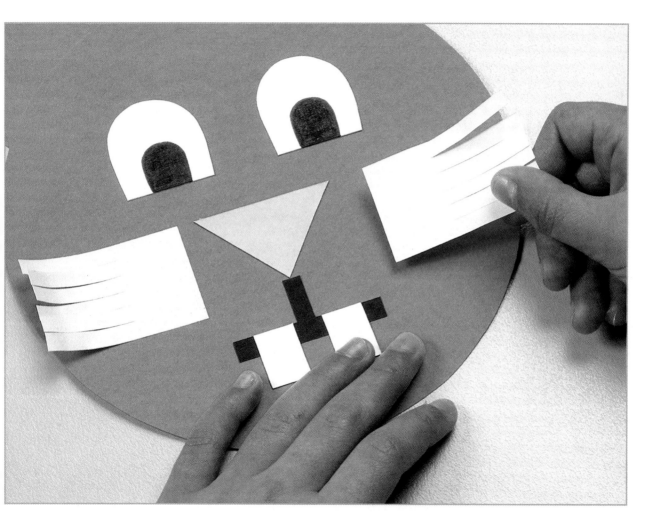

Here is the rabbit.

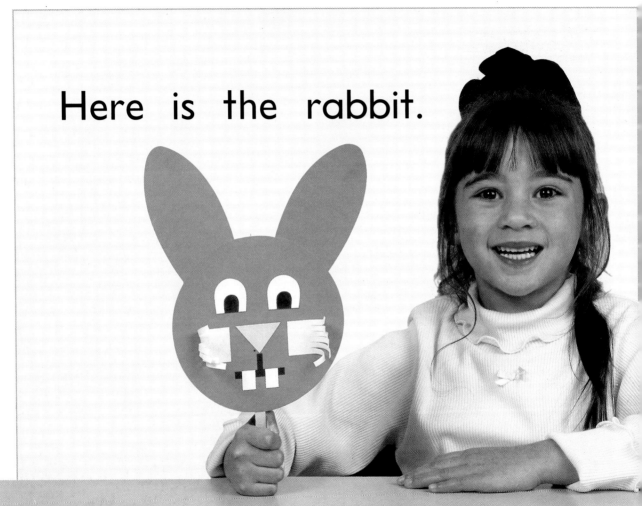